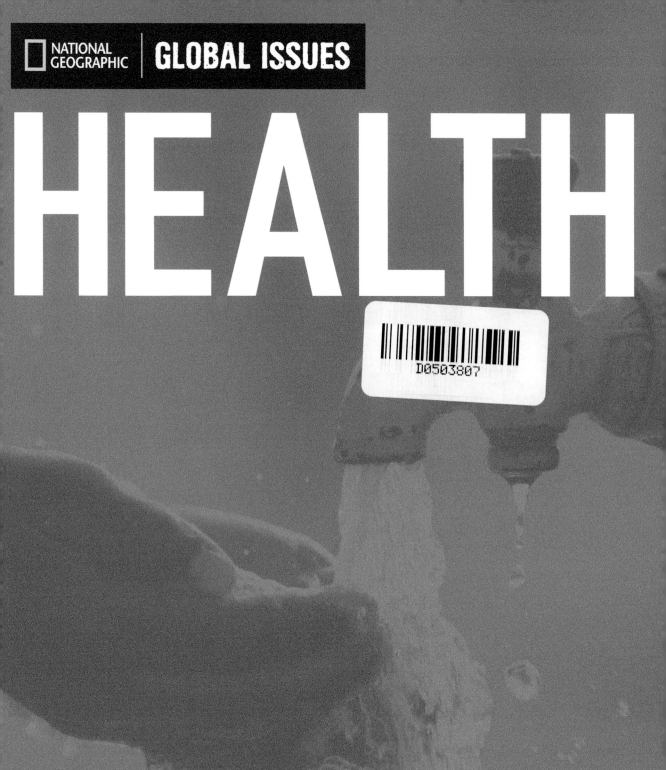

NATIONAL GEOGRAPHIC | GLOBAL ISSUES

HEALTH

D0503807

Andrew J. Milson, Ph.D.
Content Consultant
University of Texas at Arlington

Acknowledgments

Grateful acknowledgment is given to the authors, artists, photographers, museums, publishers, and agents for permission to reprint copyrighted material. Every effort has been made to secure the appropriate permission. If any omissions have been made or if corrections are required, please contact the Publisher.

Instructional Consultant: Christopher Johnson, Evanston, Illinois

Teacher Reviewers: Heather Rountree, Bedford Elementary School, Bedford, Texas

Photographic Credits

Front Cover, Inside Front Cover, Title Page ©Tim Gainey/Alamy. **4** (bg) ©Danita Delimont/Gallo Images/Getty Images. **6** (bg) ©Thomas Coex/AFP/ Getty Images. **8** (bg) Mapping Specialists. **10** (bg) ©Liba Taylor/Corbis. **11** (bl) ©Science Picture Co/Science Faction/Getty Images. **13** (bg) ©AHMED JALLANZO/epa/Corbis. **14** (bg) ©Sarah J. Glover/ KRT/Newscom. **16** (bg) ©Expa/Johann Groder/ZUMA Press/Corbis. **17** (cl) ©REUTERS/Wolfgang Rattay. **19** (bg) ©croftsphoto/Alamy. **20** (bg) ©REUTERS/Gleb Garanich. **22** (bg) ©Feliciano dos Santos. **23** (tl) ©Feliciano dos Santos. **24** (br) ©Feliciano dos Santos. **25** (bg) ©Feliciano dos Santos. **27** (t) ©St Petersburg Times/James Borchuck/The Image Works. **28** (tr) ©jo unruh/istockphoto. **30** (tc) ©Jeff Greenberg/Photolibrary/Getty Images. (bl) ©jo unruh/istockphoto. **31** (bg) ©Duncan Smith/ Photodisc/Getty Images. (tr) ©AHMED JALLANZO/ epa/Corbis. (br) ©Laurence Mouton/PhotoAlto/ agefotostock. (bl) ©Science Picture Co/Science Faction/Getty Images.

MetaMetrics® and the MetaMetrics logo and tagline are trademarks of MetaMetrics, Inc., and are registered in the United States and abroad. The trademarks and names of other companies and products mentioned herein are the property of their respective owners. Copyright © 2010 MetaMetrics, Inc. All rights reserved.

Copyright © 2014 National Geographic Learning, Cengage Learning.

ALL RIGHTS RESERVED. No part of this work covered by the copyright herein may be reproduced, transmitted, stored, or used in any form or by any means graphic, electronic, or mechanical, including but not limited to photocopying, recording, scanning, digitizing, taping, web distribution, information networks, or information storage and retrieval systems, except as permitted under Section 107 or 108 of the 1976 United States Copyright Act, without the prior written permission of the publisher.

National Geographic and the Yellow Border are registered trademarks of the National Geographic Society.

For permission to use material from this text or product, submit all requests online at www.cengage.com/permissions

Further permissions questions can be emailed to permissionrequest@cengage.com

Visit National Geographic Learning online at www.NGSP.com.

Visit our corporate website at www.cengage.com.

ISBN: 978-07362-97738

Printed in Mexico
Print Number: 08   Print Year: 2024

Pictures of HEALT

A family in Mongolia shares a meal at home. With an average life expectancy of around 68 years, children born in Mongolia have a good chance of knowing their grandchildren.

H

WHAT FACTORS AFFECT LIFE EXPECTANCY AROUND THE WORLD?

It's midnight in Paris and in the Congo. At the identical moment in both places, a baby is born. Thousands of miles apart, each new mother cradles her infant in her arms and wishes him a long and healthy life.

However, will their wishes come true? Not necessarily. Odds favor the child born in France to live so long that he meets his grandchildren and maybe even his great-grandchildren. The child born in the Congo though, may not live to adulthood.

WHO WILL LIVE? HOW LONG?

Health is a fundamental human concern. Instinctively, we want to thrive regardless of who we are or where we live.

One way of looking at health is through **life expectancy**, or the number of years a person can expect to live. Not everyone has a long life expectancy. A person born in Spain, for instance, has an average life expectancy of 81 years, while in Nigeria, life expectancy is a mere 52 years.

Why are the prospects for a long and happy life not equal around the world? Why is there such inequality?

In this book, you'll read about factors that influence life expectancy. Health isn't just about lifestyle and **heredity**, or the passing down of genes through generations. It isn't even only a medical issue. Rather, health is a reflection of society, including culture, politics, economics, and access to health care—that is, medical services.

This laboratory in France makes a medicine to prevent H1N1, a severe type of flu that can spread very quickly. Medicines such as these are expensive to manufacture and distribute and can be slow to reach remote or rural areas of developing countries.

OUTBREAKS AND BREAKTHROUGHS

Health has become a global issue. Diseases don't recognize borders. A **virus** is a tiny organism that infects living cells with disease. One of these can erupt in Malawi on Monday and can be infecting New York or Tokyo by Tuesday.

Scientific discoveries cross borders too. Sometimes it takes collaboration to find medical solutions. International teams of experts can now work together across vast distances.

Still, other factors affect life expectancy that scientists don't yet understand. What explains the population clusters of seniors around the world who live vigorous lives into their 90s and beyond? How do they stay so healthy for so long?

There are no simple solutions to health problems around the world. For example, wealth does not always guarantee good health. One measure of a country's wealth is **GDP per capita**, or the value of the goods a country produces per person. However, GDP per capita is not necessarily linked to life expectancy. Other factors may be more important to good health, such as a balanced diet, regular exercise, and being part of a strong community.

The good news is that we can advance good health everywhere on Earth. Two countries that are confronting health issues are Sierra Leone, in Africa, and Ukraine, which is in Europe. Both countries show that positive steps can be taken toward improving health.

LIFE EXPECTANCY AND INCOME

	LIFE EXPECTANCY	GDP PER CAPITA	LEADING CAUSE OF DEATH OR ILLNESS
Japan	84 years	$34,000	Stroke
France	81 years	$35,000	Cancer
United States	78 years	$48,100	Coronary heart disease
Mexico	77 years	$15,100	Coronary heart disease
Brazil	73 years	$11,600	Coronary heart disease/ stroke
India	67 years	$3,700	Coronary heart disease/ stomach illness
Russia	66 years	$15,700	Coronary heart disease
Kenya	63 years	$1,700	HIV/AIDS

Sources: *CIA World Factbook*; World Health Organization, 2012

Explore the Issue

1. **Summarize** Why is health a global issue?

2. **Compare and Contrast** How does life expectancy in countries with a high GDP per capita compare with life expectancy in countries with a low GDP per capita?

Health Concerns

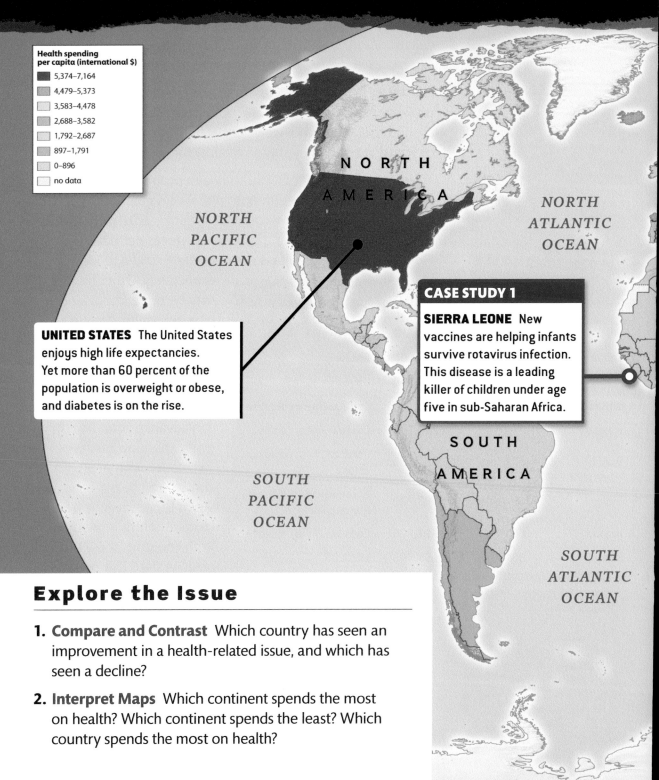

Health spending per capita (international $)
- 5,374–7,164
- 4,479–5,373
- 3,583–4,478
- 2,688–3,582
- 1,792–2,687
- 897–1,791
- 0–896
- no data

NORTH AMERICA

NORTH PACIFIC OCEAN

NORTH ATLANTIC OCEAN

CASE STUDY 1

SIERRA LEONE New vaccines are helping infants survive rotavirus infection. This disease is a leading killer of children under age five in sub-Saharan Africa.

UNITED STATES The United States enjoys high life expectancies. Yet more than 60 percent of the population is overweight or obese, and diabetes is on the rise.

SOUTH AMERICA

SOUTH PACIFIC OCEAN

SOUTH ATLANTIC OCEAN

Explore the Issue

1. **Compare and Contrast** Which country has seen an improvement in a health-related issue, and which has seen a decline?

2. **Interpret Maps** Which continent spends the most on health? Which continent spends the least? Which country spends the most on health?

ARCTIC OCEAN

EUROPE

ASIA

AFRICA

NORTH
PACIFIC
OCEAN

INDIAN
OCEAN

AUSTRALIA

ANTARCTICA

RUSSIA Russia's health care system has experienced declines in recent years. As a result, Russia is one of the few countries where life expectancy has dropped.

INDIA Infectious disease was once the main health concern in India. Now, however, changes in the Indian diet and lifestyle have made heart disease the leading cause of death.

CASE STUDY 2

UKRAINE Nearly half of all adults in Ukraine suffer from one or more chronic illnesses. Ukrainians are calling for reform of their health care system.

PHILIPPINES Infant mortality rates here have improved. The rate decreased from 42 deaths per 1,000 live births in 1990 to 23 deaths per 1,000 live births in 2010.

N
W E
S

| 0 | 1,000 | 2,000 Miles |

| 0 | 1,000 | 2,000 Kilometers |

Vaccinations in SIERRA LEO

Without a water pump, people in this remote village in Sierra Leone must travel long distances every day to collect water for their families.

SMALL BUT DEADLY

In 2011 in Sierra Leone, a country on the western coast of Africa, a panic-stricken mother rushed into a tiny health clinic with her ailing, fragile son in her arms. For four days, two-year-old Abdul had been ill with severe stomach illness.

In less developed countries, persistent stomach illness such as Abdul's is the second leading killer of children under age five. Stomach illness kills through dehydration, meaning that when the body loses too much water, bodily processes shut down. This was happening to Abdul. Health workers began to administer fluids directly into the little boy's bloodstream to replace the fluids that he had lost. Within hours, Abdul was sitting up and asking for food.

Abdul was lucky. He survived a bout of rotavirus, a tiny germ with global impact. Rotavirus causes serious intestinal illnesses. It is so common that virtually everyone has had a rotavirus infection by age five—including you. Fortunately Abdul lived, but another 1,400 children today will not.

PREVENTION AS MEDICINE

Scientists first identified rotavirus in 1973, although it has been making people and animals sick for much longer than that. Rotavirus enters the body through the mouth and then lodges in the digestive system, where it causes the stomach and intestines to become inflamed, or enlarged, causing intense pain. Rotavirus is highly **contagious**, meaning that the disease is passed easily from person to person, and the virus is also so sturdy that it can survive a long time on contaminated hands and surfaces.

These cells are the cause of human rotavirus.

Rotavirus is a particular problem in Sierra Leone and other less developed countries in sub-Saharan Africa, which lack easy access to the kind of emergency care that saved Abdul. Rotavirus can't be cured with drugs or antibiotics, and improving cleanliness or water quality does little to lower infection rates. The best way to beat rotavirus is to prevent infection in the first place. And the best prevention is a **vaccine**, which is a substance that can protect a person from a disease.

THE BODY'S OWN DEFENSES

Vaccines harness the body's natural ability to generate **antibodies**, special proteins produced by the immune system. These antibodies provide **immunity**, or protection against an illness.

While the medical value of vaccines is proven, delivering them to remote areas in less developed countries is another matter. For a vaccine to be successful, it must be inexpensive enough for developing countries to purchase and profitable enough for pharmaceutical companies to manufacture.

Because of this difficult balance, a new vaccine can take 15 to 20 years to reach a country such as Sierra Leone. A further difficulty is that rotavirus can occur in seven different strains, and each one requires a different vaccine. Furthermore, the strains that are common in Europe and the United States are not the same ones that appear in many African countries.

OBSTACLES IN SIERRA LEONE

The situation in Sierra Leone dramatically shows the difficulty of delivering lifesaving vaccines to children. It's a poor country in one of Earth's poorest regions—sub-Saharan Africa. Once, this former British colony was a vital port in the slave trade. Today, the country is working to recover from a civil war that ended in 2002 and destroyed numerous roads, bridges, and other infrastructure. The average life expectancy in the country is only 56 years.

About 60 percent of Sierra Leone's five million citizens live in the countryside, where education and health care are available only at the most basic levels. These remote areas are distant from medical resources, so delivering new medicines is difficult.

Dr. George Armah, a professor at a university in neighboring Ghana, has done research on diseases, including rotavirus, that attack a body's digestive system. He says, "The challenge has been that until today rotavirus vaccines have been much too expensive for poor countries, where health resources are scarce."

ROTAVIRUS DEATHS UNDER FIVE YEARS OF AGE		
COUNTRY	NUMBER OF DEATHS	PER 100,000 CHILDREN UNDER AGE OF 5
Sierra Leone	2,058	218
Afghanistan	25,483	474
Angola	8,788	263
Liberia	771	122
Mali	7,523	262
Nigeria	7,473	258
Somalia	5,110	317

Source: World Health Organization, 2008

Schoolgirls wait in line to receive a vaccine from a health worker. Campaigns to deliver a rotavirus vaccine can greatly reduce the number of children who die from the virus every year.

"[U]ntil today rotavirus vaccines have been much too expensive for poor countries."—Dr. George Armah

Access to vaccines can allow children in Sierra Leone to play and learn—and enjoy healthy childhoods.

HELPING AFRICAN NATIONS RECOVER

Despite the challenges, there is hope for Sierra Leone, as well as for other African countries affected by rotavirus. In 2000, the Bill & Melinda Gates Foundation launched the Global Alliance for Vaccines and Immunization, known today as the GAVI Alliance. This initiative supports vaccine development for a wide range of diseases and assists in getting them to children in resource-poor regions. The GAVI Alliance has committed billions of dollars to bringing the rotavirus vaccine to 50 million children in 40 of the world's poorest countries by 2015.

Two key innovations have boosted GAVI's success. First, GAVI is a partnership of numerous organizations involved in the improvement of global health. Second, with its many partners and donors, GAVI can provide long-term financing for the development of vaccines, which encourages more pharmaceutical companies to manufacture them, driving down costs.

PREPARING FOR A BRIGHTER FUTURE

In 2011, GAVI began to roll out the rotavirus vaccine in Sudan, another African country that faces many of the same challenges as Sierra Leone. Mass immunizations are not easy to carry out. For Sudan to begin receiving the rotavirus vaccine, entire teams of health workers had to be trained, tracking systems had to be updated, and refrigerated facilities had to be built to store thousands of vaccine doses at exactly the right temperature.

Despite these challenges, delivery of the vaccine to children was successful. Sierra Leone is among 25 other African countries identified to receive the vaccine. The rotavirus vaccine can one day save 225,000 to 325,000 young lives each year in Sierra Leone alone. One day, many more children will be as lucky as Abdul.

Explore the Issue

1. **Compare and Contrast** Why is the number of children who are victims of disease higher in less developed countries?

2. **Identify Problems and Solutions** Why are vaccines an important tool for fighting rotavirus in the developing world?

SHAPING UP in Ukrain

Ukrainian heavyweight boxing champion Vitali Klitschko now works to promote good health in his home country.

AN EPIC EPIDEMIC

Dr. Iron Fist is not happy. World heavyweight boxing champion Vitali Klitschko (KLICH-ko)—who is also known as Dr. Iron Fist—is very dissatisfied with the physical condition of his fellow Ukrainians. He has good cause. Nearly half of all adult Ukrainians suffer from one or more illnesses such as **hypertension**, or high blood pressure; **cardiovascular**, or heart, disease; diabetes; and alcoholism.

Worse, many of those who are sick are younger people who are not yet senior citizens. They should be in the prime of their life and at the peak of their productive years. Instead, more than a quarter of young Ukrainians are battling a **chronic**, or ongoing and incurable, disease. Up to seven percent of young Ukrainians have three or more chronic illnesses at once.

Vitali and Vladimir Klitschko promote fitness in Ukraine.

Ukraine is facing a serious health crisis. This health crisis among Ukraine's youth has implications for the economic and social well-being of the entire country.

WHAT HAPPENED TO HEALTH HERE?

Until 1991, Ukraine was part of the Union of Soviet Socialist Republics (USSR). Ukraine is renowned for its rich farmlands. It was the birthplace of composer Sergei Prokofiev, pianist Vladimir Horowitz, and figure skater Viktor Petrenko. And it was the site of the Chernobyl nuclear reactor explosion in 1986.

For decades, Ukraine's life expectancy kept pace with other parts of Europe, until it started to slip in the 1990s. Today, average life expectancy in the country is 11 years lower than elsewhere in the European Union. One-third of Ukrainians now die prematurely, or before age 65, and mortality is highest among working-age males. The average number of years that Ukrainians experience good health during their lives is also low.

What happened in this highly developed country with enormous resources? Why, when life expectancy has been rising in almost every other part of the world for the last 40 years, did it drop in Ukraine?

CAN SOCIETY MAKE YOU SICK?

Vitali Klitschko has an answer: Ukrainian culture doesn't encourage healthy living. For example, consider Petro Kukuy, a Ukrainian truck driver who suffered a heart attack at age 51. His job was highly **sedentary**, or inactive, for he sat behind the wheel of a truck 12 hours a day. Being inactive so much of the time for 33 years contributed greatly to his risk of a heart attack. Still, Petro didn't consider how daily exercise might improve his well-being.

Petro, unfortunately, is typical of much of the Ukrainian population. In fact, most disease-related deaths in the country result from conditions that could be prevented. Consider these facts:

- Cardiovascular disease causes nearly 40 percent of all deaths in Ukraine.
- One-third of Ukrainians ages 18 to 65 have high blood pressure.
- Thirty-six percent of Ukrainians ages 18 to 65 smoke.
- One-fifth of Ukrainians indulge in heavy drinking.

WHEN HEALTH CARE IS UNWELL

Another factor contributes to Ukraine's health issues—its health care system, which has not done an adequate job of helping people care for their health. Instead, the system has been focused on providing **acute care**, or responding to emergencies, such as strokes. The strategic importance of preventing and managing the chronic conditions that cause strokes in the first place has been overlooked.

The leaders of Ukraine are exploring ways to improve the health care system. For example, more emphasis is placed on early detection. That is, patients are regularly screened for such risk factors as obesity and high blood pressure. Currently, many Ukrainians with chronic illnesses go undiagnosed, so they don't know how to use available drugs and treatments to manage their condition.

At the same time, Ukraine's health care system can improve by emphasizing the impact that individuals have on their own health. More programs are being considered to urge Ukrainians to quit smoking and improve their diets.

A nurse examines an elderly woman in a clinic in Ukraine. Regular checkups can help detect diseases in their early stages.

71 years
Life expectancy in Ukraine in 1970

68 years
Life expectancy in Ukraine in 2009

19 years
Average age for starting smoking 40 years ago

16 years
Average age for starting smoking today

50 percent
Number of deaths of those under age 75 that could be avoided through prevention and treatment

Sources: UNICEF, 2012; World Bank, 2012.

These workers in Kiev, the capital of Ukraine, promote good health as part of a "Bike to Work" campaign.

PAYING ATTENTION TO PREVENTION

Experts suggest that efforts toward disease prevention could cut in half the number of deaths that occur before the age of 75. Public and private groups have answered the call for action. The government's economic reform efforts include initiatives to reorganize and modernize the health care system. For example, in the capital city of Kiev, the local government is opening 90 new family medical centers. These centers will allow people to see a doctor for preventive care.

In addition, Ukrainians are facing the fact that their culture has contributed to the problem. Although regulations exist against such high-risk behaviors as driving under the influence of alcohol, the regulations haven't been enforced and the behaviors are culturally accepted. In response, campaigns that deliver pro-health messages to youth are being rolled out in an effort to encourage healthy practices from an early age.

THE DOCTOR IS IN

These campaigns are where Dr. Iron Fist comes in. Besides being a world champion in boxing, Vitali Klitschko has an advanced degree in Sports Science, as does his brother Vladimir, who is also a world champion in boxing. The Klitschko brothers want to give something back to their homeland. They have formed the Klitschko Brothers Foundation, which promotes youth sports and fitness. The foundation has been opening gyms and providing sports equipment across Ukraine free of charge.

"In many countries, everyone understands that by investing in health they invest in themselves," says Vitali. He hopes to convince his fellow Ukrainians to make the same investment in longevity. It will be a tough battle—but Vitali and his brother are exceptional fighters. "Nelson Mandela said that sport can help change the world," says Vitali. "We believe the same."

Explore the Issue

1. **Analyze Cause and Effect** How have inadequacies in the Ukrainian health care system contributed to an attitude among Ukrainians that protecting their health is not a priority?

2. **Form and Support Opinions** What things can Ukrainians do to promote a healthy lifestyle?

Feliciano dos Santos

Sings Songs of Wellness

Santos, on the left, performs songs about washing hands, boiling water, and preventing disease, but he sings them in tribal languages to help get his message across.

HE'S THE GUITAR MAN

In a tiny community in southeast Africa, a crowd gathers, and the band starts jamming, everyone swaying to the beat. Do the man and his band harmonize about love, fame, or money? Hardly.

Feliciano dos Santos plays to a crowd in his native country of Mozambique.

Let's wash our hands
Let's wash our hands
For the children to stay healthy
For the uncles to stay healthy
For the mothers to stay healthy
We build latrines
—Feliciano dos Santos

This musician is not just a rock star; he is Feliciano dos Santos, a National Geographic Emerging Explorer on a mission to bolster the health of Mozambique's poor. Santos uses music to educate people about waterborne disease and the means to fight it. If his lyrics speak of simple things, such as washing hands, his vision is far-reaching. Santos believes he can advance his homeland's economic development by improving **sanitation**, the removal of trash and sewage to prevent disease.

EMERGING FROM POVERTY TO HOPE

National Geographic's Emerging Explorers Program celebrates and supports gifted young people making a difference. Whether they are scientists or storytellers, they all have the potential and the commitment to improve the world. Santos, who is an Emerging Explorer, has focused his improvement efforts on a part of northern Mozambique called Niassa. This area is one of the poorest places on Earth—and it is where Santos was born and raised. More than 60 percent of Niassa's population is **illiterate**, or unable to read or write. Few homes here have running water, and the average life expectancy is 42 years.

The World Health Organization estimates that unclean water and unsanitary conditions cause 80 percent of illness worldwide. As a child in Niassa, Santos contracted polio from contaminated water. Polio is a highly contagious disease that can cause paralysis and even death. The disease left Santos partially disabled and determined to protect others in Niassa.

THE POWER OF MUSIC TO HEAL

In 1977, a civil war broke out in Mozambique. The war claimed close to a million lives and devastated the country's economy. In the aftermath, Santos was determined to help his homeland recover. He started a band called Massukos, which means "nourishing fruit." Music, he believed, would address the psychological scars the war had left on the people of Mozambique. The music of Massukos builds on the melodies, rhythms, and dialects of Niassa.

In time, Santos and his band became famous throughout Africa and even overseas. Yet Santos kept returning to Niassa. He remained committed to helping his homeland, despite the challenges. The region remains deeply impoverished.

LYRICS AND LATRINES

In 2000, Santos founded a nonprofit organization called Estamos, with the mission of providing clean water throughout Niassa by installing water pumps plus low-cost, sustainable sanitation facilities.

The project is succeeding. Villagers have installed thousands of "EcoSan" portable bathrooms. These facilities are brick-lined to keep bacteria from infiltrating the groundwater supply. After six months of composting, the contents become fertilizer that farmers can safely use in their fields. For the first time, Niassa has a rudimentary sanitation system.

In addition, Santos is using music to teach people better **hygiene**, or the practice of keeping clean to prevent disease. One of Massukos's greatest hits is called "Tissambe Manja," meaning "Wash Our Hands." "Clean water is a basic human right, yet so many people don't have it," says Santos. "I'm using my music to be the voice of people who have no voice."

Santos speaks to children about clean water.

Explore the Issue

1. **Analyze Causes** What are some factors contributing to Mozambique's low life expectancy?

2. **Identify Problems and Solutions** Why is Santos successful at teaching people about good health practices?

"I'm using my music to be the voice of people who have no voice." —Feliciano dos Santos

Santos writes songs in traditional melodies so people can remember the message even when the music is over.

Put On a Health Fair

A health fair is an event that includes displays and demonstrations about good health habits. You will be taking part in a health fair in your classroom or school that will raise awareness of healthful practices. Who knows? You might add years to people's lives—and life to their years!

IDENTIFY

- Find out what some of the health issues are in your community. To do research, ask friends, family, and neighbors what they think are the important aspects and activities of daily life that keep them healthy.

- Identify the gaps. What habits do people need to develop to improve their health? What activities do they need to participate in?

- With three or four classmates, research and plan to take part in a health fair.

RESEARCH

- For the health fair, your group will have a booth to present information about a specific healthful practice, such as exercising regularly.

- Begin by deciding what healthful practice to present. Another example might be to show people how to shop for and prepare a healthful, nutritious meal.

- Use library resources or the Internet to collect information.

Students in Florida do jumping jacks as part of an exercise campaign.

ORGANIZE

- Plan how you will create your booth and present your information in an interesting and educational way.

- Create a visual display that shows the healthful practice. The display could be a poster, or you could even use presentation software.

- Include a demonstration. For example, one member of your group could demonstrate some simple ways in which people could build exercise into their daily lives.

SHARE

- On the day of the health fair, set up your booth and prepare for your demonstration.

- As visitors come to your booth, greet them politely, show them your visual display, and present your demonstration.

- Ask visitors whether they have any questions and provide thorough answers.

- Take photos or make a video as a record of your presentation.

Write a
TV News Story

Discoveries that improve human health are happening all the time. Some involve complicated technology, but many others don't. Some of the most important breakthroughs in health have developed from using everyday things in new ways. What are some of these discoveries? Why are they effective? Your assignment is to research and write a script for a TV news story that informs your audience about one low-cost, high-impact discovery that is improving people's health care.

RESEARCH

Use the Internet, books, and articles to research and answer the following questions:

- Why is this discovery important? Use facts to explain who is affected by it and how.
- How is this discovery similar to or different from other discoveries in this field? What makes it unique and newsworthy?
- Who are the experts in this field and what do they think are the benefits of the discovery?

DRAFT

Review your notes and write a first draft of the script.

- Start with a statement that introduces your topic clearly and previews what is to follow. Explain why you are reporting about the story from your location. Consider sharing an anecdote or presenting a dramatic fact to illustrate the discovery and engage the listener.
- The body of your script should use relevant facts, definitions, concrete details, quotations, and other information and examples. In addition, use interviews to explain why this discovery matters.
- The conclusion should follow from and support the information presented in the body of the script. Explain how this discovery could affect the listener and why it matters.

REVISE & EDIT

Read your script aloud to make sure that it is interesting and clear.

- Does the introduction clearly identify the discovery? Does it capture the listener's attention?
- Does the body of the script include facts to inform your audience about the discovery and its potential?
- Does the script end with a logical conclusion based on the facts and interviews?
- What idea will your listeners take away from the news story? Be sure that this is the most important idea.

Be sure to recheck all your facts and the spelling of all the words in your script.

PUBLISH & PRESENT

Practice delivering your script as if you were a TV news reporter. What visuals or interviews would you include? Then record yourself. Ask for permission to "air" your news story by emailing it to family and friends or by sharing it through your school's media center.

Visual GLOSSARY

sedentary

hygiene

acute care *n.*, treatment for emergency medical conditions

antibody *n.*, a special protein produced by the body's immune system

cardiovascular *adj.*, related to the heart and its vessels

chronic *adj.*, ongoing and incurable

contagious *adj.*, passed easily from person to person

GDP per capita *n.*, an estimation of the value of goods produced by each person in a country

heredity *n.*, the passing down of genes from one generation to the next

hygiene *n.*, the practice of keeping clean to prevent disease

hypertension *n.*, high blood pressure

illiterate *adj.*, unable to read or write

immunity *n.*, protection against illness

life expectancy *n.*, the average number of years a person can expect to live

sanitation *n.*, the removal of trash and sewage to prevent disease

sedentary *adj.*, inactive; remaining seated

vaccine *n.*, a substance that can protect a person from a disease

virus *n.*, a tiny organism that infects living cells with disease

vaccine

heredity

virus

INDEX

SKILLS